A Poet on the Moon

Michael Kleiza

VP

Vocamus Press
Guelph, Ontario

Written by Michael Kleiza
Some rights reserved

ISBN 13: 978-1-928171-11-9 (pbk)
ISBN 13: 978-1-928171-12-6 (ebk)

VP

Vocamus Press
130 Dublin Street, North
Guelph, Ontario, Canada
N1H 4N4

www.vocamus.net

2015

Dedication

To my partner in life, Susan, for all her support, and our children, Caitlin and Zac, the lights in my life.

Acknowledgements

Thanks to Chris Atack and Ed Nixon, fellow Rotting Poets, for helping me create the kernel of this book at The Pilot bar in Toronto, and for joining me in copious amounts of beer and cigarettes.

Thanks to Jeremy Luke Hill for his persistence and patience in motivating me to complete the manuscript.

Thanks to Sid Marty for suggesting edits and for discussing technique and cigars at the Banff Centre.

Thanks to James Clarke for editing the manuscript and for sitting down with me to discuss poetry.

Thanks to all those who validated me as a writer of poetry, including Jeremy Luke Hill, Laura Furster, John Jantunen, Jane Hastings, Leon Rooke, Melinda Burns, Laura E. Taylor, Karen Houle, Natalie Ghent, Dr. Erik Mulder, and all the people in on-line poetry groups who helped with their criticism.

A Poet on the Moon

Michael Kleiza

Acts of faith

We pass under the arch
framing a gothic Mary who
bares her sword-pierced heart
showing us the locket
that holds her faith.

It is a frigid January and my father
has decided to return to the Church
in this small Québec town.
He will last about eight weeks, and then
ease back into his bedroom
to put the rye bottle
to the glass until the early morning,
marking his racing forms with a religion
reserved for Irish priests.

I slide onto the varnished pew beside him
feet dangling, entertained
by the French priest who shuffles through
the Kyrie, robed in green under a semi-dome of sky blue
dotted with golden stars. Christ hangs alongside.
He has that beatific look torture brings
just before release:
eyes upturned to heaven and His Father.

I watch as my father rises from his seat to kneel:
the working man always subservient to God,
the company, the union,
paying dues his whole life.

At home in the evening we watch as a magician on TV
lays his half-dressed assistant
into a box of stars and moons, and
in a flourish of cloak and swords, stabs
to a sustained drum roll. Screams erupt,
the audience gasps in delight even though
they've seen the act before. And there,
once the swords are removed, she rises unbloodied
her heart unpierced, and
our faith intact.

A remembering song

I cannot tell how Eternity seems. It sweeps around me like a sea…Thank you for remembering me. Remembrance – mighty word.
   – Emily Dickinson – from Emily Dickinson Letters

This is where the swamp spread,
when in the slow time of summer
I enjoyed young days
kneeling at the fecund pond
holding down a jar that sucked water
into its wide mouth, and then found in the murk
mosquito larvae twisting and nosing
upwards for air. This is where I watched water striders
skating around bulrushes
darting over a quicksilver surface. Like six-legged Christs,
they were trick-walking their own Galilee,
using physics I hadn't yet learned.

This is where the stream ran,
when in my child's time, I walked
out of the dust from a summer's dead heat, and
with small hands, piled high the ancient slate
to block its flow.
Behind the dam, the water ceased its gurgling
and backed up in dumb pools that held horrors
for my imaginary inhabitants in the valley below.
And as suppertime approached, it always ended
with bombers flying to drop boulders
that burst holes and wreaked havoc until mother's voice
drifted from somewhere with the word "supper".

This is where the meadows were.
When behind distant houses we spent

mornings bottling bees and grasshoppers.
With burdock and milkweed in glass jam jars, I heard
the muffled buzz that caught bees make,
and the ping of grasshopper chitin
against the jar's metal lid. As the day stretched
and grew, I heard the blackbird's calls
spearing the thick hawthorn and sumac stands.
Then I drifted, cradled in the cooch grass
imagining wolf-cloud eating lamb-cloud
in a blue field sky.

This is where the raspberries grew,
when August afternoons stood windless and hot,
while mother clothed me tight against the hungry gnats.
Here, I crouched among the canes that scratched my hands
and pulled ripe and easy fruit from nippled buds,
dropping them juicy and dripping
into the enamel pot;
and, crushing some in my mouth,
I sucked out the sweetness – licked my fingers, and spit
the seeds to the ground where they would sprout
in spring, to become erect like the canes surrounding me,
their thorns a reproach to any touch.

And this is the river, where
from its banks I survey the underwater
weed beds that hold my rusted lures.
Here I stood and skipped
my hopes in stones across its rippling surface.
By this water I drank my first beer, smoked my first cigarette.

Here I walked with my mother on fog shrouded mornings
sharing a box of french fries with salt and vinegar.
This is where
I carry her ashes and spread them on water
that flows to the sea.

Photo of a farewell

The couple embraces, but the crowd faces away.
Concerned with its own losses
it does not see her hand caressing
his neck, her cheek soft in his shoulder's
harbour, dropping salt tears that mix with the shaving soap
he used this morning after love-making so complete
their bodies ended as tightly
woven as the damp sheets around them.

She has taken care to press his uniform, the creases
knife edged, and trimmed the stray hairs
on the back of his neck,
catching them in a tissue,
secreted in her purse.

She wears a smart, short-sleeved dress with a white collar
and tiny white polka dots. Her small breasts
press against his uniformed chest. And still,
they hold one another,
and all the people gathered
remain turned away.

Frog forensics: a cautionary tale

This is where I found them.
I've marked the spot
for you to find.
He must have mounted, and then
embraced her, but within the few seconds
that their amphibian love
played out on this road, the wheel
of a car must have
crushed them in their cramp.

Found on Huron's shore

This flat, scarpjawed rockscape held you,
made you recombinant
in bleached Silurian dolostone,
reefed, petrified coral, and ice-breached cliff.

Cradled, bedded in bas-relief, you were turned
to stone long before my kind – conceived
in ooze – even ventured into air.

In line and shape
you lay here now,
these remnant shores your grave.
In an ancient sea,
you schooled and swam
unaware of the squidquick eye
that tracked your path, until
in flash and strike, a lipless maw
caught and cracked you in mid-stroke
to bleed and spiral to your final rest
a half-billion years from where,
in this present place, my hands
now do their work. You are my *corpus delicti*
found from rake and shift of these remains
here, on Huron's shore.

The disappeared

Behind the living that sit
in vigil bathed
in desert sun, and the brown sandy mounds,
the pits hold a cookery of quicklime.

One of the men holds photos:
a smiling bearded man
in a white Bedouin robe,
cradling a newborn; another –
the head shot of a young woman:
the impeccably neat scarf framing
the sadness in her face
clear dark eyes that drink in the moonlight
and then perhaps, the liquid of a sun
risen gold.

Into the pit now to see
the skulls covered in taut skin
or the corpses strewn haphazard.

They have dusted a kerchiefed skull
with eyes like dried, sugary dates.
Here is the once white-robed corpse
with a ragged bundle held tight
to its chest.

The cost of a Chinese courier

Bernie spotted them first,
from his position
behind the large fronds at the edge
of the rice paddy, walking at the other
side of a glade about
a mile away.
We were looking at hitting them with mortar
until the Sarge got the idea to call in the big guns
from the ship offshore.
A bit of overkill I thought, but worth it
since Bernie had seen the big man
carrying a satchel. Bernie figured he was Chinese
because he was head and shoulders above the VC.
Radio called in the strike.
When the birds stopped whooping
we knew the big guns had fired, and we waited
for hell to break over us like a searing wind.

The first rounds screamed high overhead
hitting two hundred yards short
and plumming the paddies into dirty water feathers.

The next rounds
hit the dead silence
of the jungle where the VC were scrambling.
There was a second there where the world was a tomb.
Nothing but the sound of blood rushing through your ears.
Even the body lice stopped crawling.
And then a chorus of screams from the other side.

Slog and slog through the mud,
the story of our lives here.
Slog slog through the blood.
As we got closer, the screams
got fainter, and only moans rose
in the smashed and bloodied mouth of the jungle.
Moans that we put out like the few
remaining embers of a dying fire.

Bernie found the satchel,
still handcuffed to the courier's wrist. A couple
of bursts from the rifle tore the hand off
and Bernie's dagger popped the lock on the bag.
Inside were documents and maps
all in Chinese, with a handgun.
Wrapped in cotton, an unbroken
porcelain tea set, coloured in blue and white
with lacquered wicker cup covers. The tea set
reminded Bernie of a Chinese restaurant
he'd gone to as a kid
in Montreal.
Montreal, far away now.

We packed up and called in a chopper
to pick up the satchel. Radio
kept the gun, Bernie
kept the tea set, and the jungle
kept the dead,
swallowing them in a day.

The Spit

We pick our way over this crushed
tongue of concrete:
jack hammered sidewalks and rusted rebar where
the children imagine
exposed ribs of a Tyrannosaur, and screech
in chorus with the gulls.

Later, I sit and watch as they comb
the shoreline with a sidekicked glee,
the jetsam of scattered glass pushing
coloured suns through damp gravel.
Desperate to please, they run at me –
fill my cupped hand
with ruby, emerald, lapis.

I plunder their wide-eyed age, while
loosely tied garbage bags jammed
in the rocks snap premonitions
in a wind that breathes
only cold on my neck.

Peninsula

Here the dwarf cedars, misshapen,
and ageless as questions,
thrust tenacious roots in the Niagaran rock,
strike an old coral memory; split
the shear-cleave of the dolomite face.

Once, upon time under a shallow sea
built of brittle stars, this stone:
saucered reef and shoal, teemed
'til silty epochs glued,
and snaily ice sheets smoothed.

In our speck of human years,
now, where the scarp lolls its Silurian tongue
into the clear lake,
my hand flings full the pebbled eons,
that skip and clatter,
scatter down the cliff's sheer echo, and
sound its worn heart.

Here I plant my crippled feet,
and touch the ancient cedars.

This canvas

This canvas weighs the wild
stroke-brushed subject,
from cadmium
heavy through scourging purple and red
that bleeds into a copper sun.
Could words be as bold as this weeping art?
Where it begins subdued, there in the corner.
There! See? It catches and breathes vermilion.
Fire that rouses a blessed chorus,
colour that summons the hungry eye:
an eye if struck sightless,
would not want for more.

The sketcher

He follows a snowbound road
that leads him to where
below-zero breaths float sunlit
on the frozen air.

The old orchard,
stoops before him:
trees untended and twisted,
strangled by wild grape, yet
still appled with autumn's crop,
fruit like baubles fastened to branches,
their stems doggèd fetal chords
hooked into womb's wall.

Roadwise now, his pencil
draws memories of ladders and pickers,

pecks and bushels carried to carts.

Strokes of drunken wasps
circle the cidered air.

Spirals of gnats
fall with the autumn sun,

and a last flatbed truck heads down
a crosshatched road.

Home reno

It's his handiness
she admires, she says.
This thought bandied about the party-goers'
light talk and laughter. Later though,
she whispers of resignation:
his fugitive lovemaking rough and quick,
the twisted nipple between sandpaper fingers,
the clumsy penetration and the clockwork mechanics
scraping on the unshaved morning. She admits
her lover lost, replaced
with the snick and shhhhhhh of the tape measure,
the stepped back assessment, the accurate eyeballing,
the confident probing of breadth and height
applied to inanimate two by fours, ABS pipe,
concrete block, and wallboard. The gentle love
he once displayed, she now sees in lifting and screwing
the toilet in place without cracking a bolt hole,
levelling the shelf above the laundry tub, or
expertly inserting the P-trap into the waiting drain.

Reconstruction journalism

As we walk, he points,
"It was here...
...where I
found that part of the skull...
...with one of the eye sockets
covered in dust...
...and the eye
still in it. It is about...
...55 meters
from the explosion."

He continued, ...
"The eye had an almost mournful stare, alone
without its twin by its side.
But who can say it wasn't
a jovial, happy eye that twinkled
back, glinting a socketed impishness...Eh?"
and he chuckled that inevitable, dark humour
that dogs a city's inhabitants when the last traces of hope
have packed up and left.

After he leaves, I begin to write:
I think it would be difficult
to tell the poor wretch's state
without the context...of a mouth and lips that once, perhaps
spoke dreams, or kissed a cool cheek of a morning before rising.

...of an unshattered nose
with bridge and brow that sweated at heavy labour...
a line of jaw and chin, cheekbones high
and with the partner eye and socket...the ears, perhaps
cauliflower from a penchant to wrestle
and, two arched eyebrows,
one scarred...

I think it was here I realised
I needed this cobbled face
...written before me to feel
his last emotion
...as his cell phone rang
and the fuse sparked.

Were I her lover

In this traffic,
jammed, then
rolling slow through the morning,
on this growling Greyhound route,
with Sisyphus at my shoulder, and
the heart of Keats in my hand,
I look up from *La Belle Dame sans Merci*.
The young woman sleeping
in the seat beside me tilts her head
slightly away, her breath
passes over parted lips.
The pulse reveals a heart
under lightly freckled skin.
The couple seated in front of us
discuss the view, finance,
and the politics of the day, while
I consider the best way to place
a soft kiss
on her neck
where it throbs.

On viewing a textile

– for Marilyn

The nude with the threaded nipples
reclines on a bed of yellow stitched starfish.
Hiding in the background,
the poet embroiders a love song on Spanish leather.

Montreal

Mount Royal reclines like a woman –
all hips and breasts and
ready on a Friday night,
to take you on, daring you
to enjoy her:
Enjoy the intimacy of her alleys and back lanes
her hot summer nights with scented air tumbling over you –
outside on her cobbles. Her women,
high heels slung over their shoulders
held by their straps
barefoot in her bôites-à-chanson
sliding an arm round a boy's waist
drawing him to her as close as air –
raven hair perfumed, thick like Linden flowers
the smell of the hormonal Poplar
after the rain.
In the student ghetto
open windows in the heat
yawn like mouths with tongues;
the backrooms like throats
that groan in the night.

Remembrance 1946

On the steppes
you lay in the tall grass of Mother Russia,
your genitals
a delicacy for field mice,
your eye sockets
perfect pots for wild daisies to take root.
Traces that you were ever friend or foe,
cast to the cold Siberian wind.

Letter to a dying poet

Dear W....

Received your box of books today
With the Dale Earnhardt "Intimidator"
ball cap on top. I had to chuckle
after I read the explanation from J....

Here in the mail I also found your letter,
along with my car insurance notice
of higher premiums, and
an advertisement from the local
funeral home. How do they do it?
How do they know a person is dogged
by death – even if only by association.

There has been a snowfall overnight
and it continues this morning. Light
flakes, easy to shovel have whitened
everything that had the dirty
"thaw-look" we get here in the south.

The black-green cedars in the backyard
that cup snow in their feathered branches
are moving softly in the wind, and I see now
that enclosed in this box you have given me
work to do – some of your unfinished poems.

Your handwriting is expressive and free, unlike
my imprisoned scrawl that the Irish brothers
tried to beat out of me with their cruel wooden
rulers. But, I expect the pain I felt then is nothing to
the cancer that has riddled your massive frame.
The picture of you and J....on the couch
speaks of a happier time.

So now, as the Chinese poem of farewell says:
you wend your way slowly from this earth
in a fragile boat,
but for me there is still
the glint of your solitary lamp
on the horizon.

Summons

– for D....

Summons in a dread dawn call.
Your room-mate's panicked voice
fits the feverish red welt
expanding above the city's eastern
hi-rises.

We enter your apartment
and find you awake – night-bruised:
wild mascara'd eyes,
purple kissing your shoulder,
a thigh exposing bruises
in psychotic blue-green tinge.

You've razor'd the flesh. Dark rivulets
course between your breasts and disappear
beneath the bed sheet.

When the cops arrive
you dash naked
to the kitchen and pull out
the biggest knife
I've ever seen.

It's baby-face cop
who wrestles the knife away,
and moustache cop
who 'cuffs you;

Susan wraps the bedsheet
around your stretcher
and strapped screams.

When we walk back home, past
the convent where the girls'
hormones are dog collared and chained;

past the Forum where The Habs
will play another season of firewagon hockey;

past the children's hospital where the dying
look out from windows like bald ghosts
at the Indians in the park breathing
nail polish remover from abused plastic bags,

the morning has become too bright…
…too sunlit as we talk about you,

remembering your steamy lipsync
to Eartha Kitt's
"My Heart B'longs to Daddy" –

your birthday present
that I can still see
behind closed eyes.

The nighthawks

Diving through the moon
and the humid night air,
their breasts skimming the rooftops
within the width of a June bug,
trajectory parabolic, and
climbing to a zenith,
they set up for the next descent.

On those nights,
I knelt by my window,
listening to parental confessions.
Dad drinking beer and flicking cigarettes:
Orange ember arcing through space,
faintly glowing in the grass,
crickets in chorus.
The nighthawks in full feed, exultant.

Later, the night came to me,
cloaked in moths.
Together we drifted into sleep,
rumblings of thunder
drumming the distant air.

Sunfish

he remembers the sunfish
caught as a child:
the simple hook and hand held line –
the humid mornings
and buzzing insects, grasshoppers
in the high, brown grass
caught in cupped hands, the hook
fingered to pierce the thorax –
exiting the abdomen in a cruel upward turn
their compound eyes wondering,
their mouths spitting brown objections –
and then the wait
after the line is weighted and dropped
near the weeded
cracked concrete of this
aqueduct populated by
steel, four-legged giants
holding high tension lines
between gray angular arms –
the child now looking down
into the water, there found
the sunfish agape
at the long-legged bait
then hooked and pulled in
line over line,
hand over hand,
the flash of the scaled skin:
skipping along the water's surface.
like live silver
and then, freeing it from the hook,
storing it in the pickle jar
hidden in a hole between the concrete.

half the insect still on,
the line thrown back
and another sunfish rising, caught –
soon slipped into the bottle,
the fish vertical, standing on tails
gulping water through their gills
their eyes bulging
closing the lid he hears his mother's voice
cross the water from the stone bridge,
"Get home, Now!

He runs up the steep bank,
leaving everything behind,
the hook
the line, and
the two sunfish standing on tails
like pickles in the jar.

The bluebottle

– after Emily Dickenson

Summer kitchen bluebottle buzzing
in the dead heat. B-52 of the housefly crew,
tracing the hypnotic figure-eights
above the regular patterned white linoleum,
drone in your ears that edge-of-madness monotone,
heard once by a poetess
dying in a room
with a crowd
that had no
flyswatter.

White rhododendrons

We have reached the top of a road
with Bhuti.

The Himalayas rise in the distance:
Massiveness balanced on a tectonic plate

Our walk up 1000 meters
is in the foothills

and as we turn the corner at the top
a small stone house tumbled by the recent

earthquake scatters in our way.
A sad man and woman greet us and

we tell Bhuti to make sure to tell them
we are not from any aid agency – that

we are just on a walk through the mountains.
In the small courtyard beside their house

there are white rhododendrons like the ones
in our garden back home.

I tell Bhuti to mention this
to them, and the woman

cuts some of the flowers and gives
them to my wife and says something

which Bhuti later translates as: "Here
take these to remind you of your home, and

of us and our beautiful
frailty and despair."

Commute

On this highway,
the roadkill has been tenderized
by the 18 wheels of Peterbilts and Freightliners.
Two crows hop
from the gravel side and tear strips
off the hot asphalt in ebony beaks;

with one hand I hold
the wheel steady and
pick at the bran muffin
perched on the hand brake.

Kandahar

Mainly it's the brownness of the landscape – this,
and the blue sky and how the blood congeals
in the dust, forming a paste
on the torn flesh – that catches
your attention again, reminding
you of the first time you saw it, stark and unreal,
as you stepped off the plane, unlike
      the leafy green and sunshine of Petawawa
      shimmering in your mind after
the IED hit the LAV,
scattering nails and ballbearings
through the dusty air.

This landscape, which must be scraped and washed
from the torn and burned flesh of the dying, before
the bandages and tourniquets are applied, before
the morphine pinch blurs, before
the voices fade –
before the staunch hope
that you will make it to the Padre
with your confession.

Nothing's ever the way you think it is

With the sheets of rain coming down,
with it drenching you that way, you look
like Bogart at the train station
in Paris, having just read
the letter from Ingrid Bergman, except
Dooley Wilson's not there to push you
on the train, that,
and your fedora is missing. You don't have the
rain-soaked Mac, there is no train, or even
any train station (although this bus terminal will do).
This isn't Paris,
and you don't have the distinctive little scar
on your upper lip that you got
in a fight when you were a kid from the well-to-do
family in New York. In fact,
it is only the sheeting rain that is real.
That, and Ingrid Bergman won't be coming.

For Phil

The bird feeders offer only emptiness
to the white winter landscape.

Here is the old poet friend on TV
cashing in bottles at a Montréal dépanneur.

The birds have given up on getting food
from emptiness and the winter desolation.

The last time I saw Phil, he was playing a Pan flute
on a warm spring day at the corner of Ste-Catherine and Mackay.

The bird feeders pendulate on branches in the wind;
the snow comes and goes for most of the day.

You stood there stripped, flushed, your barrel chest breathing
        and blowing;
you curled your moustached lip, the spring air sweet on your
        mouth and the pipes.

The birds don't stop, only pass by the empty feeders
The people feed on the spring air filled with your breath and the
        flute.

Three brief encounters with Leonard Cohen

1.

I look for your earlier poems
and then remember the first time we met:

on the stairs of the Rainbow Bar and Grill
of Montreal's Stanley Street.

What humid night in summer was it? July? August?
that I stood on the sidewalk, you on the stairs

and I confessed I had bought your book
– *Let us compare mythologies that day* –

and reaching into your pocket you said:
"Do you want your money back?"
and you smiled, but the moment was lost

to the women who came and possessed you.

2.

At the Mazurka Billy F. and I drank
Polish beer and talked about blackening pages

beneath the kitschy glittering stalactite ceiling,
beside the faux Greek columns.

You came in with Henry M.
in tow and sat in a trance, burning,

while Henry fidgeted and chain smoked, and
made his way over to our table

asking for drugs of any kind. "Do you
have drugs?" Henry asks; "pot, heroin, opium, acid" –

Henry who you said was a better poet
than you'd ever be. I always

wondered about that – Henry,
whose tormented vision crept
into all our eyes.

3.

We were on St. Catherine
Amongst The Shoppers,

during a Montreal fall, where
the momentum of colour on the mountain

swirled a blaze of cold fire 'round the electric cross,
overlooking the Hassids in black

walking on Avenue du Parc.
We passed each other at Ogilvy's,

their windows an exquisite display
of autumn high fashion, while

our X-ray poet eyes briefly locked on our souls –
before moving on to other quarry.

You walked west to Buddhism. I took
to the wayward east of the city.

The news about Ginette

The memory of your passing heard
over the radio 10 years ago jolts me in my kitchen chores.

I only remember your first name
and the sketchy details of a party
where we met with friends.

Perhaps it's the shrieking tea kettle or
the crashing windowed light of morning. But I think
it's because of a broken chemical bond set to sparking
along a neural pathway like a loosened tailpipe dragging,
dislodging a memoried scene:
a dinner table haunted
with candle glow and laughing faces.

Who knew, that night we dreamed our lives
the worm was already inching into you:
            unfelt near that perfect arc closest your heart.
            Could I have told you if I'd known?

A clairvoyant,
could I have taken your hand
and traced the map on your palm
to the CBC's London bureau, that year of breaking stories:
the Falklands War, the unions
broken under Thatcher's iron rule,
and after a broadcast,
the brief note
of your death.

I remember standing there in the kitchen, when
I heard the news
much like now,
with the kettle shrieking, watching
the morning light
crash the windows.

Medical poem

You don't remember much, thank god.
They give you a shot and you
thank god again (or goddess, whatever
it takes at that point), but in the end
there's the sudden nudge, then

it's the searing pain in the upper GI,
that prods you to consciousness.
Heavy-lidded you can't escape watching
the monitor's surreal eye:
the roiling folds, a pillowed
landscape of purged bowel
and the tiny crab claw
pushing out the snaking tube,
snipping and digesting
the three larval polyps
biding their time,
waiting for the cancer
switch to flick.

Intelligent design

The instant sound of creation, everything pure
and morning's simple
spinning light arrives
out of somewhere – this the faithful know –
(the metal fish tacked to their car trunks are testament).

In a Kansas classroom
the sparking glimmer
of tongues lights the way
up a fundamental fundament:
One, and only one, equals
the christian god. No reason to rescope
monkeys here.

What is the Darwinian skullduggery
but a slow simmer in primordial soup,
an un-American crawl
through the eons of unhygienic slime.

The star formations
of low surface brightness galaxies

– for Susan

I have seen them coalesce on her bared shoulder,
when she surfaces from her deepest dreams.
Sometimes they form the inside of thighs:
spiral out from the bloom.
Sometimes they accrete on her lips,
issuing from her throat
in a whisper.

I have seen them set in a scar
that maps where children emerged:
thrashing like blind fish,
seized by their tails,
pulled from a shallow sea.

When dusk serves up her indigo bowl
with stars and a sliver of moon;
when morning tilts, and spills its contents,
over earth's edge,
I steal into her bed and place my hand
where her shoulder rises.

Image

When the horse got tired
From hauling hay
Or pulling tree stumps
Out of the hard earth
He would take a heavy chain
And beat and curse him.
My father told me this about a farmer he knew
In Quebec up around St. Lin.

Perhaps
By exposing it now I can purge myself
Of the image: the chain making that dull
Clicking sound as he lifts it and brings it down
On the animal's shoulders again, and
Again.

Reading her poems
while working in an early spring garden

– after Sharon Olds

The damp leaves dead and swollen
I coaxed and piled in the garden where
her poetry book now lay open
on the table of glass, pages
spread and ravished
by the brash west wind.

Opening her book
I tasted the ripeness of her words,
her language on my lips
like hot kisses, incisive,
where the tongue clicks the teeth
with serpent agility.

Here, in this spring garden the trees
stripped and left for dead by winter
begin their bulge to life once more:
buds that burst through the smooth skin, and
roots that pump the sticky sap through
the dark-veined trunk.

In a dream,
Jim Morrison is upstaged by the Pricecheck Girl

Morrison is dead,
              yet
                     his voice wafts
down
              in
                   sound
                              wave
after
                   sound
                              wave
                   on angel wings
        syncopated
                   through
             the
                            hyperfluorolighted
      air
of this   super
market aisle where
              we pass
the whole
            Warholesque display of
Campbell's tomato soup –
              "C'mon, baybeee
Light my fire" – sings saint Jim –
"try to set
        the night onnnnn fah"…ATTENTION SHOPPERS –
        "A blue Ford Windstar has her lights on" –
crackles through the public address system
…"OW THAT
IT WOULD BE UNTRUE" – Morrison implores

Ahead
        at the
              checkout   —
a claustrophobia
        of shopping carts
display
     toothy
        chrome
            smiles

Bongos are optional

Stage directions: The set should include a smoky '50s bistro with a stage on which a single stool stands bathed in a white hot spot light; some form of jazz is required as background, e.g., a stand up bass playing cool jazz.

Enter the poet stage right...the poet sits, looks at the crowd for a few seconds, speaks the title of the poem, and begins....

Bongos are optional
If you can find them these days
relegated to attics,
stacked on the bebop dust
78s of Dizzy and Miles
Bird squawkin' and squeakin' his
Sax
Dizzy speakin' Salt Peanuts into the mic
Salt Peanuts — Salt PEEEENuts
Miles beepin' that sweet horn
late into the hot memory
of the cool

jazz

night

somewhere in the Village
where Greenwich and Bleeker be-be-be-bop...
Johnny Staccato snapping his fingers
in a backroom beat
thick with smoke,
snappin' his fingers
to the bottom of a backbeat

bass and mute of a coronet

jazzed on that jive junk, and
blowing his brains out
into the velvet night
where out back the Subterranean
slammer Kerouac
kept typing his life on an endless roll.

Bongos are optional when
I bleat about
the bee and the bop and the birth
of the cool that haunts the ghostly lines
of every poem; about the despair
and desperation of all

Who wrote and drank,
who drew and cranked,
blew and finally gave it up
to the beat of the night.

Dark site

"SURFS UP" is printed in a loose
hand over the doorway. How is it then
that no one is waxing boards?

A poster of a bikini'd woman rubbing lotion
over her tanned flanks
is stick-pinned to the far wall –
extra pins protrude from her paper eyes
and naked torso.

A guitar twang
and four-part Beach Boy croon
wafts from the grill of a radio
on a metal desk painted
in peeling Chevy turquoise and chrome,
and you are almost back there,
on the dune's crest,
facing the ocean's ear. Dudes
that hang a pipelined ten
or goofy foot anything that moves
wouldn't know this place. No tubular
blue and white vortex
thunders shoreward to dissolve
in spent sighs
on the damp sand.

Behind the locked door
in the adjacent room, there are wet face cloths
in a neat pile, and leather straps,
hang.

Here they will tell you:

everything depends
on the face cloths
and leather straps.

The beach

All morning,
the gulls arc and soar:
white brushstrokes
against a red backdrop
of wind-carved sandstone cliffs.

We lay side by side,
the white sand warm and healing
on the curve of our backs,
the hot sun climbing above of us,
the blue chest of the sea
rising and falling at our feet.

In the afternoon, with the sun boiling
to the west, we shuffle
towards the cliffs, bodies burned,
punchy from the heat –
the smell of sun-baked seaweed
heavy in the sizzling air.

In the evening,
phosphor tentacles of jelly fish
on shore, and the perfect,
white skeleton of a gull
picked clean by the sea.

– *Port Norlunga, Australia, 1987*

A poet on the moon

– for Neil Armstrong

Here is quiet,
as the stillborn's blue lips
and airless lung –
as clear as yellowdeafening inside
the amber of a caught ant:

                      weightless
a standing wave
                      unsounded,
breathless.

Here, dust crawls over boots.

See how the marbled oceans of Earth
mount the horizon.

About the Author

Originally from Montreal, Michael Kleiza now lives in Guelph with his partner, Susan, and his children, Zac and Caitlin.

Michael's poems have been published in various anthologies and magazines. His poem "Remembrance Song" was chosen as a finalist for the William Collins Canadian Poetry Prize presented by *Descant* magazine. He has read his poetry at many venues, including The Fringe of the Eden Mills Writers' Festival, the Hillside Festival and the Art Bar in Toronto. He is an alumnus of the Wired Writing program at the Banff Centre for Creativity in Alberta.